POETRY & COMMITMENT

Also by Adrienne Rich

Poetry and Commitment *was first presented as the plenary lecture at the 2006 Conference on Poetry and Politics, Stirling University, Scotland. Adrienne Rich read a briefer version on the occasion of accepting the National Book Foundation Medal for Distinguished Contribution to American Letters.*

Poetry & Commitment

An Essay

Adrienne Rich

with an Afterword by **Mark Doty**

W • W • Norton & Company • New York • London

For information about permission to reproduce
selections from this book, write to Permissions,
W. W. Norton & Company, Inc., 500 Fifth Avenue,
New York, NY 10110

Manufacturing by Malloy Incorporated
Book design by Antonina Krass
Production manager: Devon Zahn

Library of Congress Cataloging-in-Publication Data

Rich, Adrienne Cecile.
Poetry & commitment : an essay / Adrienne Rich ; with
an afterword by Mark Doty.—1st ed.
p. cm.
ISBN 978-0-393-33103-5 (pbk.)
1. Poetics. 2. Poetry—Authorship. I. Title. II. Title:
Poetry and commitment.
PS3535.I233P64 2007
808'.1—dc22

2007002387

W. W. Norton & Company, Inc.
500 Fifth Avenue, New York, N.Y. 10110
www.wwnorton.com

W. W. Norton & Company Ltd.
Castle House, 75/76 Wells Street, London W1T 3QT

1 2 3 4 5 6 7 8 9 0

POETRY & COMMITMENT

1

Poets, readers of poetry, strangers and friends, I'm honored and glad to be here among you.

There's an invisible presence in this room, whom I want to invoke: the great Scottish Marxist bard Hugh MacDiarmid. I'll begin by reading from his exuberant, discursive manifesto called, bluntly, "The Kind of Poetry I Want." I'll offer a few extracts and hope you'll read the whole poem for yourselves:

A poetry the quality of which
Is a stand made against intellectual apathy,
Its material founded, like Gray's, on difficult knowledge
And its metres those of a poet
Who has studied Pindar and Welsh poetry,

But, more than that, its words coming from a mind
Which has experienced the sifted layers on layers
Of human lives—aware of the innumerable dead
And the innumerable to-be-born . . .

A speech, a poetry, to bring to bear upon life
The concentrated strength of all our being . . .

Is not this what we require?— . . .
A fineness and profundity of organization
Which is the condition of a variety enough
To express all the world's . . .

In photographic language, "wide-angle" poems . . .
A poetry like an operating theatre
Sparkling with a swift, deft energy,
Energy quiet and contained and fearfully alert,
In which the poet exists only as a nurse during an
    operation . . .

A poetry in which the images
Work up on each other's shoulders like Zouave acrobats,
Or strange and fascinating as the Javanese dancer,

Retna Mohini, or profound and complicated
Like all the work of Ram Gopal and his company . . .

Poetry of such an integration as cannot be effected
Until a new and conscious organization of society
Generates a new view
Of the world as a whole . . .

—A learned poetry wholly free
of the brutal love of ignorance;
And the poetry of a poet with no use
For any of the simpler forms of personal success.

A manifesto of desire for "a new and conscious organization of society" and a poetic view to match it. A manifesto that acknowledges the scope, tensions, and contradictions of the poet's undertaking. Let's bear in mind the phrases "difficult knowledge," "the concentrated strength of all our being" the poem as "wide-angled," but also the image of the poet as nurse in the operating theater: "fearfully alert."

2

What I'd like to do here is touch on some aspects of poetry as it's created and received in an even more violently politicized and brutally divided world than the one MacDiarmid knew. This won't be a shapely lecture; rather, I'll be scanning the terrain of poetry and commitment with many jump cuts, hoping some of this may rub off in other sessions and conversations.

To begin: what do I mean by commitment?

I'll flash back to 1821: Shelley's claim, in "The Defence of Poetry," that "poets are the unacknowledged legislators of the world." Piously overquoted, mostly out of context, it's taken to suggest that simply by virtue of composing verse, poets exert some exemplary moral power—in a vague unthreatening way. In fact, in his earlier political essay "A Philosophic View of Reform," Shelley had written that "Poets *and philosophers* [italics mine] are the unacknowledged" etc. The philosophers he was talking about were revolutionary-minded: Thomas Paine, William Godwin, Voltaire, Mary Wollstonecraft.

And Shelley was, no mistake, out to change the legislation of his time. For him there was no contradiction among poetry, political philosophy, and active confrontation with illegitimate authority. This was perfectly apparent to the reviewer in the *High Tory Quarterly* who mocked him as follows:

Mr. Shelley would abrogate our laws. . . . He would abolish the rights of property. . . . He would pull down our churches, level our Establishment, and burn our bibles. . . .

His poem "Queen Mab," denounced and suppressed when first printed, was later pirated in a kind of free-speech movement and sold in cheap editions on street stalls in the industrial neighborhoods of Manchester, Birmingham, and London. There, it found plenty of enthusiastic readers among a literate working- and middle-class of trade unionists and Chartists. In it, Queen Mab surveys the world's disorders and declares:

This is no unconnected misery,
Nor stands uncaused and irretrievable.
Man's evil nature, that apology
Which kings who rule, and cowards who crouch, set up
For their unnumbered crimes, sheds not the blood
Which desolates the discord-wasted land.
. . .
Nature!—No!
Kings, priests and statesmen blast the human flower. . . .

Shelley, in fact, saw powerful institutions, not original sin or "human nature," as the source of human misery. For him, art bore an integral relationship to the "struggle between Revolution and Oppression." His West Wind was the "trumpet of a prophecy," driving "dead thoughts . . . like wither'd leaves, to quicken a new birth."

He did *not* say, "Poets are the unacknowledged interior decorators of the world."

3

Pursuing this theme of the committed poet and the action of poetry in the world: two interviews, both from 1970.

A high official of the Greek military junta asks the poet Yannis Ritsos, then under house arrest: "You are a poet. Why do you get mixed up in politics?"

Ritsos answers, "A poet is the first citizen of his country and for this very reason it is the duty of the poet to be concerned about the politics of his country."

A Communist, he had been interned in fascist prison camps from 1947 to 1953; one of his books was publicly burned. For most of his countrymen he was indeed a "first citizen," a voice for a nation battered by invasion, occupation, and civil war—in poems of densely figurative beauty. As such, he was also a world citizen. His long poem "Romiosini," from its own place and era, speaks to the wars and military occupations of the twenty-first century (I extract from Kimon Friar's translation):

This landscape is as harsh as silence,
it hugs to its breast the scorching stones,
clasps in the light its orphaned olive trees and vineyards,
clenches its teeth. There is no water. Light only.
Roads vanish in light and the shadow of the sheepfold is
      made of iron.

Trees, rivers, and voices have turned to stone in the sun's
      quicklime.
Roots trip on marble. Dust-laden lentisk shrubs.
Mules and rocks. All panting. There is no water.
All are parched. For years now. All chew a morsel of sky
      to choke down their bitterness. . . .

In the field the last swallow had lingered late,
balancing in the air like a black ribbon on the sleeve of
    autumn.
Nothing else remained. Only the burned houses
    smouldering still.

The others left us some time ago to lie under the stones,
with their torn shirts and their vows scratched on the
    fallen door.
No one wept. We had no time. Only the silence grew
    deeper still. . . .

It will be hard for us to forget their hands,
it will be hard for hands calloused on a trigger to
    question a daisy. . . .

Every night in the fields the moon turns the magnificent
    dead over on their backs,
searching their faces with savage, frozen fingers to find
    her son
by the cut of his chin and his stony eyebrows,
searching their pockets. She will always find something.
    There is always something to find.

A locket with a splinter of the Cross. A stubbed-out
   cigarette.
A key, a letter, a watch stopped at seven.
We wind up the watch again. The hours plod on . . .

This was Greece speaking; today it could be Gaza or
Iraq, Afghanistan or Lebanon.

Second interview: the South African poet Dennis Bru-
tus, when asked about poetry and political activity: "I
believe that the poet—as a poet—has no obligation to
be committed, but the man—as a man—has an obli-
gation to be committed. What I'm saying is that I
think everybody ought to be committed and the poet
is just one of the many 'everybodies.' "

Dennis Brutus wrote, acted on, was imprisoned then
exiled for his opposition to the South African
apartheid regime. And he continues to act and write
in the international sphere in movements for global
economic justice. I'll read one epigrammatically terse
poem—not typical of his work but expressing a cer-
tain point:

An old black woman,
suffering,
tells me I have given her
"new images"

—a father bereaved
by radical heroism
finds consolation
in my verse.

then I know
these are those I write for
and my verse works.

My verse works. In two senses: as participant in political struggle, and at the personal, visceral level, where it's received and its witness acknowledged.

These are two responses to the question of poetry and commitment, which I take as complementary, not in opposition.

What's at stake here is the recognition of poetry as what James Scully calls "social practice." He distin-

13

guishes between "protest poetry" and "dissident poetry": Protest poetry is "conceptually shallow," "reactive," predictable in its means, too often a hand-wringing from the sidelines.

Dissident poetry, however [he writes] *does not respect boundaries between private and public, self and other. In breaking boundaries, it breaks silences, speaking for, or at best, with, the silenced; opening poetry up, putting it into the middle of life. . . . It is a poetry that talks back, that would act as part of the world, not simply as a mirror of it.*

4

I'm both a poet and one of the "everybodies" of my country. I live, in poetry and daily experience, with manipulated fear, ignorance, cultural confusion, and social antagonism huddling together on the fault line of an empire. In my lifetime I've seen the breakdown of rights and citizenship where ordinary "everybodies," poets or not, have left politics to a political class bent on shoveling the elemental resources, the public commons of the entire world into private control. Where democracy has been left to the raiding of "acknowledged" legislators, the highest bidders. In short, to a criminal element.

Ordinary, comfortable Americans have looked aside when our fraternally-twinned parties—Democrat and Republican—have backed dictatorships against popular movements abroad; as their covert agencies, through torture and assassination, through supplied weapons and military training, have propped up repressive parties and regimes in the name of anti-communism and our "national interests." Why did we think fascistic methods, the subversion of civil and human rights, would be contained somewhere else? Because as a nation, we've clung to a self-righteous false innocence, eyes shut to our own scenario, our body politic's internal bleeding.

But internal bleeding is no sudden symptom. That uncannily prescient African American writer James Baldwin asked his country, a quarter century ago: "If you don't know my father, how can you know the people in the streets of Tehran?"

This year, a report from the Bureau of Justice Statistics finds that 1 out of every 136 residents of the United States is behind bars—many in jails, unconvicted. That the percentage of black men in prison or jail is almost 12 to 1 over white male prisoners. That the states with the highest rates of incarceration and execution are those with the poorest populations.

We often hear that—by contrast with, say, Nigeria or Egypt, China or the former Soviet Union—the West doesn't imprison dissident writers. But when a nation's criminal justice system imprisons so many— often on tawdry evidence and botched due process— to be tortured in maximum security units or on death row, overwhelmingly because of color and class, it is in effect—and intention—silencing potential and actual writers, intellectuals, artists, journalists: a whole intelligentsia. The internationally known case of Mumia Abu-Jamal is emblematic but hardly unique. The methods of Abu Ghraib and Guantánamo have long been practiced in the prisons and policing of the United States.

What has all this to do with poetry? Would we have come here, from so many directions, to such a conference, if "all this" had nothing to do with poetry? (We can also imagine others who might be here if not for the collision of politics with literature.) In the words of Brecht's Galileo, addressed to scientists in a newly commercial age but equally challenging for artists: What are we working *for*?

But—let's never discount it—within every official, statistical, designated nation, there breathes another nation: of unappointed, unappeased, unacknowledged clusters of people who daily, with fierce imagination and tenacity, confront cruelties, exclusions, and indignities, signaling through those barriers—which are often literal cages—in poetry, music, street theater, murals, videos, Web sites—and through many forms of direct activism.

And this keeps happening: I began making notes for this talk last March, on a day of cold wind, flattened white light overhanging the coast where I live. Raining for almost a month. A numbing sense of dead-end, endless winter, endless war.

In the last week of March, a punitive and cynical anti-immigrant bill is introduced in Congress and passed by the House of Representatives. As most of you know, essential sectors of the Western economies depend on the low-wage labor and social vulnerability of economic refugees—especially, in the United States, from south of the border. That bill would make it a felony not just to employ, but to give medical aid, even food or water, to an "illegal" immigrant. Between the United States and Mexico, a walled, armed border would turn back those economic refugees. The hypocrisy and flagrant racism of that bill arouses a vast population. Community leaders put out the word, call the Spanish-language radio stations to announce protest gatherings. Suddenly—though such events are never really sudden—a massive series of oppositional marches pours into the streets of Los Angeles, Chicago, New York, Detroit, Atlanta, Denver, Houston, and other large and smaller cities and towns—the largest demonstrations in the history of many of those cities. Not only people from Mexico and Central America, but immigrant groups from Asia, Africa, the Caribbean, the Philippines, from Arab-American communities: families, students, activists, unions, clergy, many at risk of firing or deportation, opposing that bill. Millions of people. A working-class movement different from earlier movements. A new articulation of dignity and solidarity. And a new politicized generation growing in part out of those marches—in, for example, a coalition of young Latinos and African Americans.

Of course, there's the much larger political resistance heating up—let me simply mention Chiapas, Seattle, Buenos Aires, Genoa, Pôrto Alegre, Caracas, Mumbai, the streets of Paris and other European cities—not to mention worldwide women's and indigenous people's movements, which have never gone away—and the gay and lesbian liberation movements allied with, and often emerging from, these.

5

I hope never to idealize poetry—it has suffered
enough from that. Poetry is not a healing lotion, an
emotional massage, a kind of linguistic aromatherapy.
Neither is it a blueprint, nor an instruction manual,
nor a billboard. There is no universal Poetry anyway,
only poetries and poetics, and the streaming, inter-
twining histories to which they belong. There is
room, indeed necessity, for both Neruda and César
Vallejo, for Pier Paolo Pasolini and Alfonsina Storni,
for Audre Lorde and Aimé Césaire, for both Ezra
Pound and Nelly Sachs. Poetries are no more pure and
simple than human histories are pure and simple.
Poetry, like silk or coffee or oil or human flesh, has
had its trade routes. And there are colonized poetics

and resilient poetics, transmissions across frontiers not easily traced.

Walt Whitman never separated his poetry from his vision of American democracy—a vision severely tested in a Civil War fought over the economics of slavery. Late in life he called "poetic lore . . . a conversation overheard in the dusk, from speakers far or hid, of which we get only a few broken murmurs"—the obscurity, we might think now, of democracy itself.

But also of those "dark times" in and about which Bertolt Brecht assured us there would be songs.

Poetry has been charged with "aestheticizing," thus being complicit in, the violent realities of power, of practices like collective punishment, torture, rape, and genocide. This accusation was famously invoked in Adorno's "after the Holocaust lyric poetry is impossible"—which Adorno later retracted and which a succession of Jewish poets have in their practice rejected. I'm thinking now not only of post–World War II poets like Celan, Edmond Jabès, Nelly Sachs, Kadia Molo-

dowsky, Muriel Rukeyser, Irena Klepfisz. I'm also
thinking of contemporary poems in a recent collection
from Israel that I've been reading in translation: *With
an Iron Pen: Hebrew Protest Poetry, 1980–2004,* ignited
by the atrocious policies and practices of Israel's occu-
pation of Palestine. There, poems of dissonant, harsh
beauty, some thrusting images of the Occupation into
the very interior of Israeli domestic life:

. . . I open the refrigerator door
and see a weeping roll,
see a piece of bleeding cheese,
a radish forced to sprout
by shocks from wires
and blows from fists.
The meat on its plate
tells of placentas
cast aside by roadblocks. . . .
   —Aharon Shabtai, "The Fence," trans. Peter Cole)

—or suggesting how the poem itself endures its own
knowledge:

The poem isn't served meat and fruit
on a silver platter at night,
and by day its mouth does not long
for a golden spoon or communion wafers.
Lost, it wanders the roads of Beit Jala,
sways like a drunk through the streets of Bethlehem,
seeking you along the way in vain,
searching for your shadow's shadow in the shrubs.

Close to the breast, the soul sits
curled up like a boy in a sleeping bag
dry as a flower bulb buried in the middle of the throat.
Then the poem feels it can't go on any longer
wandering towards the refugee camp,
toward the fugitives' cradle
in the Promised Land's heavy summer
on the path to disaster

> —(Rami Saari, "Searching the Land,"
> trans. Lisa Katz)

Do poems like these "work"? How do we calculate
such a thing on a day when Israel is battering its way
into Gaza, cluster-bombing Lebanon? Like the activist,
the poet (who may be both) has to reckon with disas-

ter, desperation, and exhaustion—these, too, are the materials.

And in such a time—when water is poisoned, when sewage flows into houses, when air becomes unbreathable from the dust of blasted schools and hospitals—poetry must gasp for breath.

But if poetry had gone mute after every genocide in history, there would be no poetry left in the world, and this conference might have a different theme: "The Death of the Poem" perhaps?

If to "aestheticize" is to glide across brutality and cruelty, treat them merely as dramatic occasions for the artist rather than structures of power to be revealed and dismantled—much hangs on the words "merely" and "rather than." Opportunism isn't the same as committed attention. But we can also define the "aesthetic" not as a privileged and sequestered rendering of human suffering, but as news of an awareness, a resistance, that totalizing systems want to quell: art reaching into us for what's still passionate, still unintimidated, still unquenched.

Poetry has been written off on other counts: (1) it's not a mass-market "product": it doesn't get sold on airport newsstands or in supermarket aisles; (2) the actual consumption figures for poetry can't be quantified at the checkout counter; (3) it's too "difficult" for the average mind; (4) it's too elite, but the wealthy don't bid for it at Sotheby's. It is, in short, redundant. This might be called the free-market critique of poetry.

There's actually an odd correlation between these ideas: poetry is either inadequate, even immoral, in the face of human suffering, or it's unprofitable, hence useless. Either way, poets are advised to hang our heads or fold our tents. Yet in fact, throughout the world, transfusions of poetic language can and do quite literally keep bodies and souls together—and more.

Two items from recent news. One is a headline from the *San Francisco Chronicle* of July 17, 2005:

WRITING POETRY WAS THE BALM
THAT KEPT GUANTANAMO PRISONERS
FROM GOING MAD

The story follows a Pakistani, Abdul Rahim Muslim Dost, arrested in Afghanistan and held without charges in the American detention camp at Guantánamo. There he wrote thousands of lines in Pashto, translated Arabic poetry into Pashto, at first scratching lines with his fingernail into Styrofoam cups. His brother and fellow inmate is quoted as saying that "Poetry was our support and psychological uplift. . . . Many people have lost their minds there. I know 40 or 50 prisoners who are mad."

These men, detained as terrorists (released after three years), turned to poetry in the depths of Guantánamo to keep themselves sane, hold onto a sense of self and culture. So, too, the Chinese immigrants to California in the early twentieth century, detained in barracks on an island in San Francisco Bay, traced their ideograms of anger and loneliness on the walls of that prison.

But poetry sometimes also finds those who weren't looking for it.

From the Israeli newspaper *Ha'aretz* of November 7, 2004, comes an article by David Zonsheine, a former commander in the Israeli Defense Force who became organizer and leader of the anti-Occupation movement within the IDF, the Courage to Refuse. Zonsheine comes by chance upon some lines from a poem of Yitzhak Laor and finds that,

Reading these lines a moment after a violent month of reserve duty, which was full of a sense of the righteousness of the way, was no easy thing. I remember that for one alarming moment I felt that I was looking at something I was forbidden to see. What this thing was I did not know, but on that same Friday afternoon I went out to look for every book by Yitzhak Laor that I could find in the shops.

Zonsheine continues,

The sense of mission with which I enlisted in the IDF was based . . . on . . . the painfully simple message that we shall not allow the Holocaust of the Jews of Europe to repeat itself no matter what the costs, and when the moral price became more severe, the sense of mission only increased . . . I am a freedom fighter . . . not an occupier, not cruel, certainly not immoral. . . .

Something in Laor's texts spoke to me about the place
inside me that had been closed and denied until then. . . .

Here I am, 28 years old, returning home from another
month of reserve duty in Gaza and suddenly asking
myself questions that are beginning to penetrate even the
armor of the righteousness . . . in which they had dressed
me years ago. And Laor's strong words return to echo in
my ears: "With such obedience? With such obedience?
With such obedience?"

Ever since I refused to serve in the territories and the
Ometz Lesarev (Courage to Refuse) movement was
established, I have returned again and again to Laor's
texts. . . .

. . . The voice is that of a poetic persona through whose
life the "situation" passes and touches everything he has,
grasping and refusing to let go. The child, the wife, the
hours of wakefulness alone at night, memory, the very
act of writing—everything is political. And from the
other extreme, every terror attack, every act of occupa-
tion, every moral injustice—everything is completely
personal.

29

. . . This is . . . a poetry that does not seek parental approval or any other approval, a poetry that liberates from the limitations of criticism of the discourse, and a poetry that . . . finds the independent place that revolts and refuses."

Did Laor's poetry "work"? Did Zonsheine's commitment "work"? In either sense of the word, at any given moment, how do we measure? If we say No, does that mean we give up on poetry? On resistance? With such obedience?

"Something I was forbidden to see."

6

Critical discourse about poetry has said little about the daily conditions of our material existence, past and present: how they imprint the life of the feelings, of involuntary human responses—how we glimpse a blur of smoke in the air, look at a pair of shoes in a shop window, at a woman asleep in her car or a group of men on a street corner, how we hear the whir of a helicopter or rain on the roof or music on the radio upstairs, how we meet or avoid the eyes of a neighbor or a stranger. That pressure bends our angle of vision whether we recognize it or not. A great many well-wrought, banal poems, like a great many essays on poetry and poetics, are written as if such pressures didn't exist. But this only reveals their existence.

It's sometimes taken that politicized emotions belong solely to the "oppressed" or "disenfranchised" or "outraged," or to a facile liberalism. Can it still be controversial to say that an apparently disengaged poetics may also speak a political language—of self-enclosed complacency, passivity, opportunism, false neutrality—or that such poetry can simply be, in Mayakovsky's phrase, a "cardboard horse"?

But when poetry lays its hand on our shoulder, as Yitzhak Laor's poem did for David Zonsheine, we are, to an almost physical degree, touched and moved. The imagination's roads open before us, giving the lie to that slammed and bolted door, that razor-wired fence, that brute dictum *"There is no alternative."*

Of course, like the consciousness behind it, behind any art, a poem can be deep or shallow, visionary or glib, prescient or stuck in an already lagging trendiness. What's pushing the grammar and syntax, the sounds, the images—is it the constriction of literalism, fundamentalism, professionalism—a stunted language? Or is it the great muscle of metaphor, drawing strength from resemblance in difference? The great muscle of the unconstricted throat?

I'd like to suggest this: If there's a line to be drawn, it's not so much between secularism and belief as between those for whom language has metaphoric density and those for whom it is merely formulaic—to be used for repression, manipulation, empty certitudes to ensure obedience.

And such a line can also be drawn between ideologically obedient hack verse and an engaged poetics that endures the weight of the unknown, the untracked, the unrealized, along with its urgencies for and against.

7

Antonio Gramsci wrote of the culture of the future that "new" individual artists can't be manufactured: art is a part of society—but that to imagine a new socialist society is to imagine a new kind of art that we can't foresee from where we now stand. "One must speak," Gramsci wrote, "of a struggle for a new culture, that is, for a new moral life that cannot but be intimately connected to a new intuition of life, until it becomes a new way of feeling and seeing reality and, therefore, a world intimately ingrained in 'possible artists' and 'possible works of art.'"

In any present society, a distinction needs to be made between the "avant-garde that always remains the same"—what a friend of mine has called "the poetry of false problems"—and a poetics searching for transformative meaning on the shoreline of what can now be thought or said. Adonis, writing of Arab poetry, reminds Arab poets that "modernity should be a creative vision, or it will be no more than a fashion. Fashion grows old from the moment it is born, while creativity is ageless. Therefore not all modernity is creativity, but creativity is eternally modern."

For now, poetry has the capacity—in its own ways and by its own means—to remind us of something we are forbidden to see. A forgotten future: a still-uncreated site whose moral architecture is founded not on ownership and dispossession, the subjection of women, torture and bribes, outcast and tribe, but on the continuous redefining of freedom—that word now held under house arrest by the rhetoric of the "free" market. This ongoing future, written off over and over, is still within view. All over the world its paths are being rediscovered and reinvented: through collective action, through many kinds of art. Its elementary condition is the recovery and redistribution of the world's resources that have been extracted from the many by the few.

There are other ghostly presences here along with Hugh MacDiarmid: Qaifi Azami. William Blake. Bertolt Brecht. Gwendolyn Brooks. Aimé Césaire. Hart Crane. Roque Dalton. Rubén Darío. Robert Duncan. Faiz Ahmed Faiz. Forugh Farrokhzad. Robert Hayden. Nazim Hikmet. Billie Holiday. June Jordan. Federico García Lorca. Audre Lorde. Bob Marley. Vladimir Mayakovsky. Thomas McGrath. Pablo Neruda. Lorine Niedecker. Charles Olson. George Oppen. Wilfred Owen. Pier Paolo Pasolini. Dalia Ravikovitch. Edwin Rolfe. Muriel Rukeyser. Léopold Senghor. Nina Simone. Bessie Smith. César Vallejo.

I don't speak these names, by the way, as a canon: they are voices mingling in a long conversation, a long turbulence, a great, vexed, and often maligned tradition, in poetry as in politics. The tradition of radical modernism, which crosses and recrosses the map of poetry. The tradition of those who have written against the silences of their time and location. Without it—in poetry as in politics—our world is unintelligible.

A friend asks: And what about Baudelaire, Emily Dickinson, T. S. Eliot, Gerard Manley Hopkins, D. H. Lawrence, Montale, Plath, Ezra Pound, Rimbaud, Rilke, Wallace Stevens, Yeats? In the context of that conversation their poems flare up anew, signals flashing across contested, even infected waters. I'm not talking about literary "intertextuality" or a "world poetry" but about what Muriel Rukeyser said poetry can be: *an exchange of energy,* which, in changing consciousness, can effect *change in existing conditions.*

Translation can both betray and make possible that exchange of energy. I've relied—both today and in my lifelong sense of what poetry can be—on translation: the carrying-over, the trade routes of language and literature. And the questions of who is translated, who are the translators, how and by whom the work is done and distributed are also, in a world of imbalanced power and language, political questions. Let's bear in mind the Triangle Trade as a quintessential agony of translation.

In his *Poetics of Relation* Édouard Glissant meditates on the transmutations opening out of that abyss of the Middle Passage. He writes of the Caribbean that,

*though this experience [of the abyss] made you, original
victim . . . an exception, it became something shared,
and made us, the descendants, one people among others.
Peoples do not live on exception. Relation is not made up
of things that are foreign but of shared knowledge. . . .*

*This is why we stay with poetry. . . . We know ourselves
as part and as crowd, in an unknown that does not ter-
rify. We cry our cry of poetry. Our boats are open, and
we sail them for everyone.*

Finally: there is always that in poetry which will not be
grasped, which cannot be described, which survives
our ardent attention, our critical theories, our class-
rooms, our late-night arguments. There is always (I am
quoting the poet/translator Américo Ferrari) "an
unspeakable where, perhaps, the nucleus of the living
relation between the poem and the world resides."

The living relation between the poem and the world:
difficult knowledge, operating theater where the poet,
committed, goes on working.

Santa Cruz, California
2006

Afterword by Mark Doty

Recently, I listened to a prominent literary critic speaking to a group of young poets—many of them my students—in a graduate writing program. He told them that if they didn't like the way things were being run in the country, the thing for them to do was to devote some time each week to organizing voters and advocating social change, but to be sure to keep their political concerns out of their work, as it would do "terrible damage to their poetry, as it did to the poets of the 1970s." My first reaction was to think that my students should *be* so lucky for their work to be informed by such a clear, compassionate purpose. I was taken aback by the critic's absolute certainty, his lack of a more nuanced or complex position—and then I thought, well, critics have probably been giving precisely this advice to poets since the beginning of literary time, and poets have been ignoring them and continuing to allow whatever was central to them to shape their poems.

Adrienne Rich has been brilliantly and challengingly pursuing her passions for some five decades now, and if my students seek an example of what happens when a poet follows what matters most to her, they need look no further. Her lived commitment to questioning and revealing the structures of power and how we live within them turns out to be "the huge rockshelves" under her work, as Rich put it once in a great poem called "Transcendental Etude." These rockshelves are the ground upon which she has founded a sustaining poetic, a life's work—but also the ground upon which to build her profoundly generous gift to others: a deep, public valuing of the common life.

Walt Whitman wrote, in the preface to the first edition of *Leaves of Grass,* that the proof of a poet was that he'd be "absorbed into the affections of his country as firmly as he has absorbed it." A year later, after he'd sold maybe two dozen copies of his book, he revised that sentence: "The proof of a poet," he wrote, "must be sternly deferred until he has been absorbed into the affections of his country." Adrienne Rich's volumes of poems and collections of essays, I hardly need tell you, have been showered by every award available to an American writer, including the Bollingen Prize and the Wallace Stevens Award. This evening she receives the Medal for Distinguished Contribution to American Letters from the National Book Foundation, joining Gwendolyn Brooks as the only poets ever to be so honored. Her poems are foundational texts of our time, and, in the future, when readers want to understand the great reconsideration of gender and power that reshaped American life, it is to Rich's poems that they will turn. Now I suppose this means that she has been "absorbed" in the way Whitman meant, but in truth that has not been her goal; she has remained a gadfly, a vigilant witness somehow both at the center and in the margins of her age. When the Clinton White House invited her to come to Washington to accept a National Medal for the Arts, she declined to accept an award from an administration she saw as abusing its powers; I probably don't need to tell you that the current administration has not been forthcoming with an invitation. Her restless empathy for those not in positions of power—women, the poor, laborers, queer women and men, the immigrant—is the ethical basis of her art. And if the critic in his position of aesthetic purity believes that poems suffer from it, then perhaps we've labored under a hobblingly narrow definition of poetry, a fiction of a realm in which words in their harmonies and shadings operate at a remove from the world, in some sacred grove. That idyllic glen, if it ever existed, was entered by human traffic long ago, and where people live, inequity resides. Rich has spent her entire career gazing into that difficult truth. In Adrienne Rich's strong hands, the poem is an instrument for change, if we can see into the structures of power and take on the work of making a dream—"the dream of a common language"—an actuality. As Whitman did, she calls us toward the country we could be, though she insists that we acknowledge the country we are.

There is a beautiful essay of Rilke's called "The Vocation of the Poet," in which the German poet describes a journey to Egypt sometime toward the beginning of the twentieth century, and how he saw there, on the Nile, an old-style boat rowed by many rowers. At its front sat a man with a drum, facing the oarsmen, setting their pace. But in front of him sat someone else, a singer, whose job it was to face into the direction the boat was heading, singing into the future.

That is what Adrienne Rich has been doing over the long, brave haul of a remarkable career, and through that singing she has helped us to see where we are and where we're heading. Her words, given and given again, have helped to make that future what it will be; she has lent a voice to what our best selves might make. Like Whitman, Rich has created her audience; like her predecessor Muriel Rukeyser, she has spoken into a silence and readers have risen to her words awakened, changed.

Please join me in saluting an essential American writer.

Bibliography

Adonis. *An Introduction to Arab Poetics.* Trans. Catherine Cobham. Austin: University of Texas Press, 1997.

Brutus, Dennis. *Poetry and Protest: A Dennis Brutus Reader.* Ed. Lee Sustar and Aisha Karim. Chicago: Haymarket, 2006.

Cárdenas, José. "Young Immigrants Raise Voices, and Hopes." *St. Petersburg* (Florida) *Times,* May 13, 2006.

Coghlan, Thomas. "Writing Poetry Was the Balm That Kept Guantanamo Prisoners from Going Mad." *San Francisco Chronicle,* July 17, 2005.

Foot, Paul. In *International Socialist Review* no. 46 (March–April 2006).

Franklin, H. Bruce. "The American Prison and the Normalization of Torture." *http://www.historians againstwar.org/resources/torture/brucefranklin.html.*

Glissant, Édouard. *Poetics of Relation*. Trans. Betsy Wing. Ann Arbor: University of Michigan Press, 1997.

Gramsci, Antonio. *Selections from Cultural Writings*. Ed. David Forgacs and Geoffrey Nowell-Smith. Trans. William Boelhower. Cambridge, Mass.: Harvard University Press, 1985.

Holmes, Richard. *Shelley: The Pursuit*. New ed. New York: New York Review of Books, 2003.

Lai, Him Mark, Genny Lim, and Judy Yung. *Island: Poetry and History of Chinese Immigrants on Angel Island, 1910–1940*. San Francisco: Hod Doi, 1980.

MacDiarmid, Hugh. *Collected Poems of Hugh MacDiarmid*. Ed. John C. Weston. New York: Macmillan, 1967.

Mayakovsky, Vladimir. *How Are Verses Made?* Trans. G. M. Hyde. New York: Jonathan Cape/Grossman, 1974.

Ritsos, Yannis. *Yannis Ritsos, Selected Poems 1938–1988*. Ed. and trans. Kimon Friar and Kostas Myrsiades. Brockport, N.Y.: BOA, 1989.

Scully, James. *Line Break: Poetry as Social Practice*. Foreword by Adrienne Rich. Willimantic, Conn.: Curbstone, 2005.

Stocking, Marion. "Books in Brief." *Beloit Poetry Journal* 56 (Summer 2006).

Vallejo, César. *Trilce*. Trans. Clayton Eshleman. Intro. by Américo Ferrari. New York: Marsilio, 1992.

White, Elizabeth. "1 in 36 U.S. Residents behind Bars: U.S. Prisons, Jails Grew by 1,000 Inmates a Week from '04 to '05." Associated Press, May 22, 2006.

Whitman, Walt. *Walt Whitman: Complete Poetry and Collected Prose*. Ed. Justin Kaplan. New York: Literary Classics of the United States, Library of America, 1982.

Zonsheine, David. "A Personal and Political Moment." *Ha'aretz,* November 7, 2004.

Permissions

51

Adrienne Rich's recent books include *The School Among the Ruins: Poems 2000–2004* (2004), *Arts of the Possible: Essays and Conversations* (2001), and *What Is Found There: Notebooks on Poetry and Politics* (2003). She edited Muriel Rukeyser's *Selected Poems* for the Library of America. Her work has received the Lenore Marshall/*Nation* Prize, the Wallace Stevens Award, the Bollingen Prize in Poetry, and the National Book Foundation's 2006 Medal for Distinguished Contribution to American Letters, among other recognitions. *Telephone Ringing in the Labyrinth: Poems 2004–2006* will be published in October 2007. Since 1984 she has lived in California.